THE BORDER FANCY CANARY

ITS BREEDING, REARING AND MANAGEMENT

By

JAMES PATTERSON

Fifth Edition

"CAGE BIRDS"
DORSET HOUSE, STAMFORD STREET, S.E.1

MADE AND PRINTED IN GREAT BRITAIN FOR
THE PUBLISHERS, POULTRY WORLD LTD., AT
THE CHAPEL RIVER PRESS, ANDOVER, HANTS
7.50

PREFACE

EVERY year, hundreds of new breeders take up the breeding and exhibiting of the popular Border Fancy Canary, and the need of a standard work for their guidance has always been widely felt. The main object of this booklet is to help the beginner by telling in simple language how to proceed on the road to success in breeding and exhibiting. By making clear to him what to do and what to avoid, the information contained in these pages, will, it is hoped, save the novice from making mistakes and impressing faults in his strain that will take years to stamp out.

The advice given is the result of a lifetime's experience, both from a breeder's and an exhibitor's point of view, and I trust that my readers may derive from the book as much pleasure and enjoyment as I have found in writing it.

JAMES PATTERSON

CONTENTS

THE BORDER FANCY CANARY

CHAPTER I

INTRODUCTORY

THOSE whose minds are imbued with a love of Nature as she attires herself in varying garbs, changing as each season comes round, will find in the breeding of the Border Fancy Canary a congenial hobby and one which will keep them fully occupied.

To breed, keep in health, and exhibit the bird leaves no idle time on hand. There is ample scope with this bright little bird for all who delight in a graceful outline, and variation in colour, type and markings. The Border's outstanding beauty and delicacy of form must appeal to everyone, and all who love a rarity will find contentment in breeding any of the varieties— be they Clears, Marks, Greens or Cinnamons.

To establish a notable strain requires the study of a lifetime so as to breed them to conform to the standard laid down by the Border Fancy Canary Club. To breed and exhibit a perfect bird one must be brimful and bubbling over with enthusiasm. Among the breeders of each variety the keenest enthusiasts will be found at the top, each one having in his, or her, mind's eye a true conception of every point in detail.

Therefore all who take up this interesting variety as a hobby, and wish to be successful, require to give it close study, work hard, and be very careful and painstaking in everything they do. To the careless and unthoughtful comes failure. Such failure I have found invariably due to the fancier's lack of observation.

I find real bird lovers the most human of men and women. The reason is no doubt that birds are so fascinating, so attractive and pleasing to the sight. A first-class bird on the show bench arrests our attention and compels the admiration of every one, whether exhibitor or visitor to the show.

To the exhibitor the eye takes precedence over the ear, and few exhibitors take more than a passing interest in the song of their birds. To others, the song of the canary is first and foremost. For these, the Border Fancy will hold his own with any variety as a songster, and being such a hardy and contented little chap, with due care and attention will live for years, and greatly help to liven up the drab monotony of everyday life in the household.

Breeders and exhibitors will find sound knowledge a great asset and mostly the result of hard work in years gone by. Therefore, the beginner must not expect to reach the top in one season or two. We who delight in the hobby, are only partly paid in cash. We receive also a certain amount of experience and a big share of disappointment.

The Technical Points

1. Head, small, round and neat-looking.
2. Bill, fine.
3. Eyes, dark and bright.
4. Neck, rather fine and proportionate to head and body.
5. Back, well filled and nicely rounded.
6. Gentle rise over shoulders.
7. Chest, also nicely rounded, neither heavy nor prominent.
8. Wings, compact and carried close to body.
8a. Wings, just meeting at tips.

9. Legs, of medium length, fine and in harmony with other points.

9a. Legs, showing little or no thigh.

10. Size, not to exceed $5\frac{1}{2}$ inches measured in the usual way.

11. Plumage, close, firm, and of fine quality, free from frill.

12. Tail, close packed and narrow.

12a. Tail, nicely rounded and filled in at the root.

13. Position, semi-erect, standing about an angle of 60 degrees.

14. Carriage, gay and jaunty, with a fine free pose of the head.

CHAPTER II

ORIGIN AND HISTORY

THE origin of the Border Fancy Canary is still left in doubt, although many articles and letters attempting to fix its ancestry have been published in the general and Fancy Press. Previous to the year 1826 we have only circumstantial evidence to go by. Certainly we have proof that the domestic Canary existed in this country early in the eighteenth century, and was then known as the " Canary Serin ".

The former part of the name indicates its country of origin and the latter its true name, meaning Serin Finch. The original colour, we are told, was between green and grey. From the drawing of the Serin Finch we may see that our " Wee Border " still maintains its true outline and characteristics in general more than any other variety of its progeny which appears on the show bench. We have therefore to thank the original breeders

5

for much that is graceful and beautiful in the Border Canary. When we think of it we cannot wonder. Nowhere in my younger days could you find keener fanciers than the shoemakers and weavers of the Border Counties of Scotland. Amongst them, the bird was bred in great numbers and what they did not know about the breed in general was not worth learning.

" Common Canary " or " Cumberland Fancy "

Strange to say each town or village had a distinct variety, some favouring clears, others the even marked variety, and a very few greens. Cinnamons at that time were very rare. The bird was known then as the Common Canary in Scotland. The bird is said to have been first introduced into England by a shoemaker who took his birds with him from Langholm into Cumberland.

About that time the variety began to spread from its stronghold throughout all the counties on both sides of the Border. Its outstanding charm when exhibited at the local shows, captivated all who saw it, but its chief supporters were still to be found around the Border Counties of Dumfries, Roxburgh and Selkirk in Scotland.

From the year 1882 to 1890 (when the Border Fancy Club was formed) a very long, keen and heated controversy took place in the Fancy Press of that time between the breeders in Scotland and England. The bird was exhibited in Scotland as the " Common Canary " and in England as the " Cumberland Fancy ", each country claiming to be its birthplace. The late Mr. J. B. Richardson, of Dumfries, writing under the *nom-de-plume* of " Veritas ", clearly proved from facts and figures, that it was bred in Scotland long before it was known in England.

Formation of the Border Club

Perhaps an account of the formation of the Border Fancy Canary Club may be both instructive and interesting to readers and to any members who are not quite clear concerning its origin. On June 23rd, 1890, a circular was sent out by the late Mr. Thomas Arnot, of Hawick, to all secretaries of shows asking them to elect a delegate to represent each district at a meeting to be held in Hawick on July 5th to decide on a suitable name for the variety and to discuss the desirability of forming a club to draw up a standard of points and further the interests of the breed.

A large number of delegates attended and appointed Mr. Richardson chairman. After a friendly discussion a resolution was passed disapproving of the names " Common Canary " and " Cumberland Fancy " and declaring that on and after that date the bird should be known as the Border Fancy Canary. A club was then formed and called " The Border Fancy Canary Club ". Mr. J. B. Richardson was appointed president, and Mr. Thomas Arnot, of Hawick, secretary, with a committee of six.

Mr. Richardson was president from the year 1890 until 1913.; Mr. George W. Brown, of Leith, from 1913 to 1915 ; Mr. M. Jamieson, of Hawick, from 1915 to 1919 ; Mr. J. Patterson, of Chirnside, from 1919 to 1923 ; and Mr. J. Lumsden, of Edinburgh, from 1923 to 1926, being succeeded by the Acting-President, Mr. W. S. Clark, of Irvine. The secretarial office was held by Mr. Thomas Arnot from 1890 until 1892, and by Mr. M. Jamieson,

Hawick, from 1893 to 1913. Mr. W. B. Smart, of Loanhead, was then elected, and he was followed by Mr. D. Whitelaw, of Glasgow, and J. Binnie, who is the present secretary. That the club has been fortunate in its officials may be gathered from the fact that while in 1890 the membership was 43, to-day members number approximately 700.

For the formation of the club and the drafting of the rules, Messrs. Richardson and Arnot were largely responsible, and I can confidently say that without their enthusiastic leadership the Border Fancy Canary would never have reached the high state of perfection to which it has attained. From both of these gentlemen, who were close personal friends of mine, I derived much of the knowledge which forms the basis of this book.

" A Wonder of the Fancy "

At a meeting at Langholm in 1891, held to select a model from the leading birds shown that season, the two leading judges appointed were Mr. Bell, of Jedburgh, and Mr. Davidson, of Dumfries. The bird finally chosen was shown by Mr. McMillan, of Langholm. This model is one of the wonders of the Cage Bird Fancy, and a portrayal of the bird was for some years contained in the book of rules as a guide for the aspirant to follow and attempt to equal in his breeding operations.

In the year 1893 the club procured a challenge cup by subscription. The conditions of competition decided upon were that it must be won three times in succession, or four times in all. In 1893 it was won by Mr. Bell, of Ecclefechan, with a clear buff cock ; and by Mr. Welsh (Hawick) in 1894, with a yellow clear cock. Mr. Downie (Carlisle) won it in 1895 with a clear yellow hen. Mr. Henry Bennet, of Kelso, then won it outright three years in succession, each year with a clear bird. Clear birds at that time were superior to the variegated and dark varieties. In 1895 a motion that a uniform or standard cage be adopted was rejected.

Colour Feeding Barred

In the same year at a special meeting, a motion that colour feeding should be entirely abolished was proposed, and also that all birds showing type and quality should count before good marking. At the general meeting in 1896, held in Carlisle, after a long discussion it was agreed to let the colour question remain over at present. In 1897 the question of a standard cage was again brought forward, but again rejected.

In the year 1900 a proposal to bar colour feeding was once more rejected, but in 1901 it was agreed to take a plebiscite of all the members. The vote resulted as follows :—

In favour of colour feeding .. 21
Against 111
_____
Majority 90
_____

At that time the membership stood at 134. This finding has stood since that date.

Since that time the membership has increased yearly until to-day it is one of the largest specialist clubs.

CHAPTER III

DESCRIPTION AND POINTS

HAVING kept and exhibited all other varieties, I can confidently recommend the Border Fancy as one of the most jaunty and charming of any of the Canary family. I have had more pleasure from the Border than from any other variety and have been a slave to its charm for the last thirty-five years.

The Border is now, so far as Scotland and about 50 per cent. of English Counties are concerned one of the most popular varieties. That is not to be wondered at. For it is hardy, is easily bred, and its close fitting, silky feather, of pure level colour, its dapper figure, its jaunty carriage, and the gay air and easy movement with which it goes from perch to perch fairly takes the beginner's heart by storm.

Even older breeders of other varieties are leaving their first love, and taking up the Border Fancy. Where a songster is kept you will find in nine cases out of ten it is the little cheeky Border, delighting its owners with its musical song and charming ways.

The essential points of the Border Fancy are now widely known. Type and quality come first. Colour and markings are a second consideration. Each point has to be carefully bred for, and is only reached through study and a wise selection when pairing up the stock birds. The first step the novice who decides to take up this variety should make is to join the Border Fancy Canary Club. The Secretary will be delighted to hear from fanciers wishing to join.

In considering the standard of excellence and accurate description of the points in detail of the Border Fancy Canary, it must be borne in mind that the grand essentials are type and quality. Without these it is worthless.

The Standard of Excellence

The general appearance is that of a clean-cut bird lightly made, compact, proportionable, sprightly, close-feathered, smallish-sized Canary, showing no tendency to heaviness, roughness, frilling, flatness or dullness, giving the impression of fine quality and symmetry throughout.

Head.—Small, round and neat-looking. Bill fine, eyes dark and bright, neck rather fine and proportionate to head and body.

Body.—Back well filled and nicely rounded, running in almost a straight line from the gentle rise over the shoulders to the point of the tail. Chest also nicely rounded, but neither heavy nor prominent, the line gradually tapering away to vent.

Wings.—Compact, and carried close to the body and just meeting at the tips.

Legs.—Of medium length, showing little or no thigh, fine and in harmony with other points, feet corresponding.

Size.—Not to exceed 5½ inches in length, measuring in the usual way.

Plumage.—Close, firm, and fine in quality, presenting a smooth, glossy, silky appearance, and free from frill or roughness.

Tail.—Closely packed and narrow, being nicely rounded and filled in at the root.

Colour.—Rich, soft, and pure, as level in tint as possible throughout; extreme depth or hardness, such as colour feeding gives, are objectionable in this breed and should be discouraged. Red fed birds distinctly debarred. Birds with one or two marks to compete in ticked classes; and clear bodied birds, with foul legs or bills, to compete in clear classes. Birds with three or more distinct marks to compete in variegated classes; one or two marks in green or cinnamon classes constitute a foul bird; three marks constitute a variegated bird.

Position.—Semi-erect, standing at an angle of 60 degrees.

Carriage.—Gay and jaunty, with a fine free pose of the head.

Health.—Condition and cleanliness shall have due weight.

Now I think it will be gathered from the above rules of the club what constitutes a good Border Fancy Canary, and once you breed one with all the points already described, you will have something that will open the eyes of your friends, something to warm your heart, a joy to look upon, a credit to yourself as the breeder, and a pride to any judge you exhibit under.

I know from my own experience there is nothing gives a judge more pleasure than a good class all nearly equal in type and quality, for it provides something to recall with pleasure years afterwards. Classes at all the principal shows are well represented by typical birds.

Within recent years the craze for size has hampered many breeders, and caused a lot of ill-feeling and discontent among the members. To see these over-sized birds in the prize list is a great mistake, and breeders, exhibitors and judges who favour them break one of the most clear and binding rules : " No bird must exceed 5½ inches ".

To my mind, once a bird gets over the standard length it loses much of its general style and sprightliness. For a bird to be slow, awkward and clumsy in action is one of the worst faults it can have.

Standard of Points

The standard of points allowed as given by the rules already mentioned is as follows :—

	Points
Head and Neck	10
Body and Back	15
Wings	10
Legs	5
Tail	5
Plumage and Condition	15
Colour	10
Position	10
Carriage	10
Health and Cleanliness	10
Total	100

The chief faults to guard against in show and stock birds are the following :—

Large heavy beaks, especially those with a tendency to point downwards.

Large flat heads, or heads pinched and narrow before the eye.

Thick necks, giving the impression of body and head being held tight together, showing no shoulder, and freedom of the head when moving.

Long or ungainly flights and frayed at tips, or not meeting and covering the back.

Tails carried either too high or too low. Fish tailed.

Too long in legs, too high in thighs, or wide between feet.

Large and coarse, too thin in front or vice versa.

Frilling in front, or at thighs.

Too large in body and long in side.

Flat across the perch, long and loose in feather, washed out or uneven in colour.

Wing Carriage Faults

All these faults should be avoided as far as possible, either in a stock or show bird. In those birds showing the wing carriage at fault the wing will be found too long which makes them look heavy-sided and out of proportion with regard to other points.   Others will be found crossing badly at tips.

Then there are others with wings which are thin in the outer flights, the outside edges too being more or less frayed. Others do not cover the back at all, only meeting at the tips, and leaving a deficiency up the back with the rump feathers exposed. To be perfect the wings must meet all over and be laid close to back, covering the side and showing an open roundness, though not so close to the body as to give the impression that they are drawn. Many a rare good bird in other points fails here, and this matter should always be kept well in hand when pairing up, of which I shall speak later.

Another bad fault, and one to which, to my mind, some judges do not pay enough attention, is when a bird is not finished off at the root of tail, commonly termed "nipped at vent". There is not sufficient feather behind the legs to give that gradual taper which finishes off a good bird in conjunction with a close, compact and well carried tail.

Some may say it is impossible to breed all birds with a close, compact and narrow tail, but once you give it careful study a few years will suffice to root out this fault.

Another point which breeders must be careful to watch closely is the tendency in some birds to be rough in either body feather, or on the feather at thighs, and upwards towards the vent and waist. These faults look very untidy, and I find when once established in a strain they are difficult to breed out again.

Coming to the head, this should be neat, small and round—not flat over skull or before or behind the eye. No bird with a flat head should ever be " in the money " in a class where there are others to choose from. The same remarks apply to the neck. One may see birds winning when the neck and head are firmly joined together without the slightest tendency to rise over shoulder.

We cannot have freedom in action of head unless there is that nicely cleaned neck, both above and below so well brought out and seen in the model sent out by the Border Club. Last, but not least, comes the question of colour, a question so important that it requires a chapter of its own.

CHAPTER IV

THE QUESTION OF COLOUR

THIS is a great factor with some judges, which indeed it should be, as I find it is difficult to maintain good colour in some strains. Their richness of plumage seems to fade more and more each generation, and some of them become as many-coloured as Jacob's coat.

The reason of this is not far to seek. If you examine such birds in your hand you will find that the feathers are carrying more colour at the outer web end than down the web, leaving the longer feathers exposed, which will look pale beside the shorter feather on body, head and neck. Nothing looks worse than a bird patchy in colour, and this trait must be bred out or the strain discarded.

Much has been written on the vexed question of colour-feeding. This, I am afraid, will always remain a subject of controversy. Many birds I have seen shelved as being " colour-fed " where I could not find any trace. Others, again, have won under suspicion. Breeding for colour is one of the most interesting studies that one can take up. A lot is talked and written about colour breeding by people who have not the slightest knowledge of blending the shades together to get the desired level colouring so well brought out on some of the birds exhibited.

Double Yellowing

If in yellows there is a tendency to fade in colour, I have found that double yellowing one pair for a season helps to establish more depth. For this purpose select as rich a coloured cock bird as you have amongst your stock. The shorter the body feather the better, providing it has a rich glossy (not dull) colour.

Mate him up to a yellow hen pale in colour, but with the tint of colour level throughout (what is termed a lemon-coloured hen). See, however, that she is typical in every point, and nice and short in leg. Double yellowing has a tendency to produce birds not so heavily feathered at waist and at thighs, thus making the bird look much longer in leg than it really is.

Another way to improve colours is by introducing green blood, but I am not an advocate of this method, especially if breeding for Clears. Birds marked on thighs, backs, and legs will appear in your clear strain for generations afterwards. Indeed, I may say it is impossible to breed out. It may perhaps not appear in a brood, and you may congratulate yourself thinking you have got rid of it, but next season you will find it break out again and where least expected.

These leg, thigh, and base of tail markings are very minute, and might escape your eye at home, but in a show, where the birds seem to expose the thighs more, the judge sees the ticks, and your cage is marked " wrong class ". When such birds are shown in clear classes he has no other alternative.

Double yellowing has a tendency also to reduce the size of body, and where the neck is too thick it will also work wonders.

Buffs Worth their Weight in Gold

From a double-yellow pair you will get some buff birds. Stick to the buff hens from this cross. If typical and up to standard in weight, they are worth their weight in gold to fix the level tone of colour so much desired by all.

" Double-buffing " is another means to the desired end, and can be used to advantage, but one must know the strain of birds to introduce into this cross, which has a tendency to make birds a shade stouter in body and thick and short in neck, but can also be used to advantage to fix quality and shortness of feather.

In this mating I pay particular attention to the soundness of colour. The cock must have a neat small head, be nice and thin in neck both above and below, and the quality of feather must be of the best. The hen also must be level in colour throughout, perfect in type, and not too large. In fact, they are better to be both undersized, but from a good strain. No cross can bring up better colour in your yellows next season when mated the usual way, yellow to buff or vice versa.

I prefer this to any other cross ever used as a colour producer. You get birds far more level in colour than from either greens or variegated birds. From a double-buff pair the progeny will be all buff.

23

These, mated to yellows, will increase the number of your yellows in the next season providing the right birds have been used.

At one time, when I was at the height of my career as a breeder, and had more time on hand, I could produce 80 per cent. yellows from any given pair, and I can justly claim to have then bred the best yellows (both cocks and hens) ever produced and shown by any one breeder.

CHAPTER V

MATING FOR MARKINGS

WE now arrive at another very important point in regard to markings. No variety of markings is more difficult to obtain than the even-marked, and when once obtained they are even more difficult to maintain.

For the uninitiated I may point out that there are six defined points on which, alone, technical " marks " may exist. First there are the two eye marks or two wing marks. Specimens possessing these are termed two-pointed birds. The six-pointed have two eye, two wing marks, and one dark feather each side of tail. The ideal mark is the four-pointed bird with eyes and wing markings only.

The eye-markings to be perfect should be pear-shaped with the eye in the centre to taper off behind eye so as to correspond to that in front. The wing markings should be alike in number of dark feathers. I do not like to see a heavy-marked wing, and prefer from four to six dark feathers in the inner flights. This is quite enough and looks more graceful and pleasing.

Where the wing is almost composed of dark feathers they give to the eye the impression of heaviness, spoiling the side view and making a bird look hollow in back just where the markings join.

The Beautiful Even Mark

The evenly-marked Border is without doubt well worthy of all the attention we can bestow upon it, as it is really the beauty of them all, and at shows the most handled and admired. Some twenty odd years ago it was the ideal of all breeders, and nothing could please one better than to see some of the beauties then shown. I had my share of them, and I know from personal experience how proud one became when winning a good class of even marks.

Unfortunately, in former years when the variety was more sought after than has lately been the case, it had the unenviable reputation of being more often the outcome of skilful manipulation on the part of the exhibitor rather than being what nature intended it to be.

In those days many judges made their awards for good markings alone, and exhibitors being only human, wished to give them what they wanted. Where a feather could come out here and there without being detected so as to improve the markings, it was done.

Other judges I have found do not care a straw for technical markings. If they get a bird of their particular type, markings are considered last of all. All, however, who have attempted to breed a perfect even-marked bird, will know what great care, patience and luck combined it takes to produce a winner with good eye and wing markings balanced.

Since the Border Fancy Canary Club drew up their special list for patronage shows, the even-marked class is now (unless at some of the larger shows) a thing of the past. In my opinion if they are properly shown they will win against any other birds wherever they are placed as they are the very acme of the breeder's art and may be termed *the Ideal*.

There is no fixed rule or successful method whereby we can assure ourselves that we can breed the largest percentage of the young from any given pair, even or unevenly marked. Indeed, the breeder must know his stock, its full pedigree, where inclined to throw light or dark markings for three or four generations back, before he can be sure of breeding even one good and perfectly marked young bird each season.

But when the stock has been handled for some years, one begins to know and find out each peculiar turn the markings now and again take. You feel more confident in pairing up, and can thereby introduce or subtract the dark blood just where you know attention is required, although at times your best thought out plans are apt to go wrong.

The Use of Variegated

Many a time when you think you should breed a champion, you will find the blood does not blend in the markings. Just when you want to build them up the progeny comes more or less variegated. The latter I have found most useful in building up your eye markings. You have far more chance to breed a good mark from those heavily variegated specimens when mated to a clear-bred from a good marked strain.

The great mistake the young fancier or beginner so often makes lies here. His first thoughts are : " Only let me get two evenly-marked birds together and I am sure to succeed, and shall have most of the young like their parents ".

The Young Fancier's Disappointment

His disappointment is great when he finds the progeny nearly all green or variegated. And this is when he gets perplexed, and very often sells his most useful stock birds thinking them entirely useless, whereas if he had kept them and mated them to clears or ticks they might have produced a good blend of markings with some winning marks amongst the progeny.

Here, however, is where the amateur has a good chance to start well and cheaply. If he is in touch with a breeder of good marked birds and knows the stock, he should buy one of these variegated birds and select for its partner a clear, or tick, bred from a good marked strain. Then ten to one he will breed a good mark in every nest. They may not be evens or perfectly marked, but the breeder runs a chance of a good uneven.

I find that each bird has a tendency to throw the markings more like its grandparents than its own parents. For this reason I advocate the breeding of the variegated or greens with clears rather than with an even mark. If you pair a clear to a lightly marked bird you may expect a few marked birds, but I have found this cross to throw the eye-markings light, and these take a lot of making good when once you allow them to deteriorate. However, if eye-markings are poor, you must persevere and introduce mates with more dark blood to those birds that fail in this respect, say a variegated showing distinctly the ideal or large eye-markings.

The breeding of the evenly marked bird is a perplexing question. Why it should be so difficult in Canaries is one of Nature's hidden mysteries. It can be done with poultry and pigeons of all varieties which have a fixed standard of markings, and

I am sure there is a fortune awaiting the man who can establish a strain of even marked birds that will give twenty-five per cent. of their progeny with the true markings.

Type must not be Forgotten

Another point you must not neglect is the type of your marked birds. We all of us at times are so taken up with the markings that we may be termed a " little marked on the brain ", and when pairing up our birds we only think of these points, forgetting type until we breed a good marked bird which, to our chagrin, we find deficient in type, so much so, indeed, that it is quite out of the question to place it on the show bench as an exhibition specimen. If we had paid a little more attention to former pairing, we should have saved ourselves the trouble we are now faced with, i.e., of again introducing birds of type along with markings.

In this mating the best method is to pair a clear cock from a typical strain to a heavily variegated hen showing the eye-markings distinctly. Always try and avoid head marked birds, or you will find the marks whether on the crown or back of the head very hard to breed out, and always apt to reappear many years afterwards.

Let it be clearly understood I only advocate the above cross with a clear when a suitable mate with marked blood is not available. Clear breeders have not the markings to contend with, with the result they can pay more attention to type. Hence my reason for introducing the clear when type is lacking in marked birds.

Among the progeny of your marked pairs you will get a number of lightly-marked and ticked birds. The lightly-marked birds will be exhibited in the unevenly marked classes. These include all five-pointed birds, that is, those marked with two eye and wing marks and a feather in tail, and also all three-pointed birds. To the latter class belong birds with both eyes and one wing marked, or one eye and both wings, or again, birds marked on both wings and side of tail. The uneven or variegated class is set aside for birds marked on any other part of the body.

At most of the larger shows a class is also given for heavily variegated birds that must be three parts dark. From your matings you will also get a number of ticked birds which are those with either one or two small marks on either eye or on any other part of the body.

The Border Fancy Club limits the marks to a size that can be covered by a sixpenny piece, also allowing three dark flight feathers. Breeders may expect a few ticked birds amongst the progeny of their clear pairs.

CHAPTER VI

GREENS AND CINNAMONS

THE Green Border Canary up to about the year 1905 was very much neglected. Even the leading shows only gave one or two classes for them. Those classes then mostly took in the self Cinnamons. Even with their aid the classes were but poorly filled, and strange to say the winners were almost all yellows.

The judges then somehow did not favour the buff birds. The late Mr. J. B. Richardson, of Dumfries, and the late Mr. T. Arnot, of Hawick, who, as I have said, were two of the most enthusiastic breeders and exhibitors at that time, then intervened.

In 1905 Mr. Richardson guaranteed a class for Greens at Hawick, and Mr. Arnot one at the Scottish National in Edinburgh. Both were well filled and some grand birds were shown.

In my articles on the Border Fancy Canary which appeared in *Cage Birds* at that time, I expressed the hope that both classes would be well filled with a record entry, as such an event might be the means of adding a few more admirers to the ranks of green breeders which were then so very small. That hope has been abundantly fulfilled.

At a recent show held by the Scottish National there were four classes for Greens and four for Cinnamons, with an average of 18 birds per class. This shows what rapid strides the Greens and Cinnamons have made in the last twenty years, and one cannot wonder.

A Striking Appearance

No bird, to my mind, has such a striking appearance as a good grass green Border, provided it is level in colour, distinct in pencilling, and not showing any bronze on its body or on wings. Young birds have a more or less bronzy colour on their wing butts, but this is allowed for by judges.

Many also show a tendency to run light in throat, down thighs, and root of tail. All such blemishes have to be avoided in the colour of greens, and birds possessing them must have strict attention paid to their mating.

If you have a bird showing any tendency to the above faults, and which to your mind is equal in type and quality to your ideal, it is a pity to discard it from your green strain. When paired to a heavily-variegated bird with a dash of cinnamon blood established in it, the bronze colouring disappears.

From this cross you cannot expect all self Greens. A few variegated and foul Greens will appear, but by pairing those back to a good Green you will breed birds showing better markings, more quality of feather and greater depth of colour.

Select the most typical and best-coloured, also those showing the pencilling most prominently down the breast and flank markings, as after crossing in the variegated the progeny has a tendency to go light in throat, breast and flank. Pair back to a bird bred from double greens and you may hope to have a fair amount of true-coloured grass Greens.

Some breeders also believe in double buffing a pair for a season, which also helps to tone down the bronze colouring.

There is not the slightest doubt that green breeding takes up a great amount of time, and requires careful selection and attention. The average fancier who has only his spare time and accommodation in his bird-room for a limited stock, must almost relinquish the breeding of other varieties, as Greens are very little use to introduce into either marks or clears.

A breeder must have at least four pairs to keep him in stock, so as not to run them too " sib " (that is, too closely related) and even with that number he has great difficulty to keep clear of inbreeding. He must be buying often to avoid it, and introducing fresh blood into his stock so often that unless he has some particular friend of whose stock he knows the full pedigree, it is frequently a very disappointing job.

The " blood " may not blend, and this leaves him many a time at his wits' end how to get rid of it again. Therefore to keep a strain together requires something like a dozen pairs.

Cinnamons

Years ago, Cinnamons had no class allotted to them at shows, they being always exhibited amongst the Greens. At that time I called attention to the neglect of this variety, although it had taken the fancy of many breeders, and I prophesied that we should at some future date see a class specially allotted to them.

Then one year I guaranteed a class for them at two shows, and although these classes were not well filled, the number shown gave me great encouragement.

The following season the classes filled and paid for themselves. Since then they have never looked back, and at many shows the full classification is granted. Such classes are very heavy, and some splendid birds are on view at each show, forming a great attraction for visitors.

In the early days, only a very few Cinnamon hens were shown. Usually each Green breeder strove hard to get one of these Cinnamon hens, nearly all of which were very dull and pale in colour.

The First Cinnamon Cock

Previous to the year 1893 no Cinnamon cocks in this variety were shown, and the first one out caused quite a sensation among breeders, as in most of our minds the idea was firmly fixed that a Cinnamon cock could not be bred. This rarity caused us to use our thinking powers, and many a long discussion took place at shows.

I believe I am right in saying that the late Thomas Arnot arrived nearer to the truth than any of us by saying the parents of the bird had been sib-bred ; in other words that both parents had cinnamon blood in their veins. We then realised that we had not enough cinnamon blood in our strains and so introduced birds known to have cinnamon blood, and at least four fanciers bred a Cinnamon cock that year.

By exchanging birds with cinnamon blood among ourselves we established strains, and within a few years very few fanciers' rooms were without a pair of Cinnamons. The result was they improved in colour and became the rage of every fancier worthy of his salt.

I have found them also the most useful for toning down the feather where there is a tendency to coarseness, either in clears or marks. Indeed, at that time there was hardly a bird in my room which had not a large percentage of cinnamon blood well established, and I never knew any bad effect to result.

I can, therefore, confidently recommend it to tone down any coarseness, and to produce that nice silky feather so much sought after and which we all admire.

In breeding Cinnamons, which must also conform to the rules, the main point is colour and pencilling. The former must be level throughout, both above and below, without any trace of harshness, and minus any dirty drab or greyish tinge.

Improving the Colour

The pencilling must be very similar to that in Greens, but must be a little finer at flanks, back and side. In breeding Cinnamons, never pair two birds for colour alone. Type here is a strong factor, as the Cinnamon somehow has a tendency to run light in weight in front and often rather narrow over shoulder.

To improve the colour a double yellow cross works wonders. But I find the best method is to pair a heavily-variegated Yellow cock with good type and colour to a self Yellow hen of good size and substance. The variegated blood, if of the right colour

GREENS AND CINNAMONS

tone, seems to give a much clearer tone
in the succeeding pairings.

Never double yellow unless you have
the right material in hand, as it has the
tendency to make the ends of feathers thin
and, therefore, easily spoiled, especially
flights and tails, and also a tendency to
breed birds high in legs.

In double buffing, look out for tight
feather in both birds as the progeny has
a tendency to throw birds a little long in
feather. It is not so noticeable in the first
cross but may be expected later. Select
the cock as rich in colour as possible.

You will find in some buff cocks the
colour giving a slight tinge of yellow,
particularly at head and shoulder. This is
the bird you want and it should be mated
to a hen as typical as possible. The object
of a double buff cross is to increase the
size and substance in your stock.

However, if a fancier does not understand
his stock it is advisable to stick to yellow
and buff, or vice versa.

Cinnamon Marked Birds

In the Cinnamon mark we have the gem
of all the varieties ; but it is a bird that

is not at all easy to rear. The cause of this I have never been able to discover, and from correspondence with other breeders, I find they have had the same experience as myself.

If you are breeding a mixed variety of marks, and have a Cinnamon mark in the nest, ten to one that is the bird that dies. Strange to say, I find pink-eyed birds survive where the marked bird dies. Many a good one have I lost. Cinnamon blood has a great tendency to produce good markings.

When you *do* come on a good Cinnamon mark at a show, or in a bird-room, you will never forget the lovely, tight-fitting feather of superb quality, shining like satin. When put down clean their charm is hard to resist.

In breeding Cinnamon marks, the birds must be similarly handled as for Green-marked breeding, but the clear bird must be pink-eyed. Two lightly-marked birds may be paired together with more confidence than in Green-marked breeding, as the cinnamon blood is inclined to throw them lighter than their parents.

Sometimes one must introduce a Green cross if it is desired to improve a weak point in either type or colour. For this cross, I prefer a heavily variegated yellow green-marked hen mated to a self cinnamon buff cock. From this cross, unless the variegated hen has cinnamon blood, the cinnamon-marked progeny will all be hens. These hens, when paired back to a cinnamon-marked cock will produce cinnamon-coloured birds, both cocks and hens, with a few green-marked birds also.

Peculiarities of Cinnamon Blending

The peculiarities of blending cinnamon blood may be stated as follows :—

(1) A cinnamon-coloured cock, be he a self cinnamon mark, or a pink-eyed clear, or even a cinnamon-bred green-marked, mated to a non-cinnamon-bred hen, will not produce any cinnamon sons. Any cinnamons, either clear, pink-eyed, selfs, or marked, will prove to be hens.

(2) Should a cinnamon-coloured cock be bred, it is proof positive that cinnamon blood exists in the mother as well as the father. On the other hand, a cinnamon hen, be it either clear, pink-eyed, self, or

marked, cannot produce a cinnamon-coloured chick unless the bird paired to her had cinnamon blood in him.

(3) To breed Cinnamons, both cocks and hens, it is necessary to have the cinnamon blood in both parents. It will thus be seen how easy it is to get a cinnamon-coloured hen. The slightest trace of cinnamon blood in a cock bird will give a cinnamon-coloured hen, but you must have at least fifty per cent. cinnamon blood in both parents to produce both cocks and hens.

I think I have said enough to show the intricacies of cinnamon crossing.

The same applies to all the White varieties of Canaries. Here again we have a lovely bird, in the Snowy-white Border, and one that is a great attraction at shows. Within recent years I have had the pleasure of owning two of another variety, namely, a cinnamon-marked hen with green marking also.

Another one came into my possession, but had the reverse marking, namely, a green-marked hen with a cinnamon mark on head. In neither of these could the pedigree be very clearly proved. I had a

44

number of birds sent from a friend, who bred a bird similarly marked, but unfortunately they escaped out of the birdroom window.

What I wished to establish was a strain of birds that would produce the two colours—cinnamon and green marks showing on the same body. So far ill-luck has prevented me from succeeding with this cross, but I intend to keep on with the attempt.

With cats it is quite impossible to get a three-coloured male, and it would be interesting to find out if the same applies to Canary breeding.

CHAPTER VII

STARTING A STRAIN

BEFORE purchasing any breeding stock get to know, by reading up the advertisements and show reports in *Cage Birds* those who are fairly successful with their exhibits. Attend all the cage bird shows held within your district. There, I have no doubt, some particular birds will take your fancy.

Try and get an introduction to the owner of these birds; have a chat with him, and find out how they were bred. Ask him how many birds he has for sale of the same strain and type, with particulars and price.

Don't grudge a few shillings extra for a good bird or pair of birds. You had far better keep few but good, if your means are limited. Get as many birds as possible from him, allowing him to pair them up for you, seeing he will understand how they are bred and how they will throw their progeny. You will thus save yourself unnecessary trouble.

Some may say this is giving him too free a hand and trusting too much to his honesty. But always bear in mind there are many honest fanciers among Canary breeders and it is better to put your faith in one good man than a number.

If you go about buying a bird here and another there, although to all appearances these birds may look well matched, you will find the blood does not blend, and it will take you many years to breed a winner. In some instances one may succeed, but this very rarely happens.

A lot of trouble and expense can be avoided by a happy first selection. If not satisfied with all the progeny, let the breeder know, and he will doubtless be pleased to assist you with his knowledge as to how the parents were bred. In the following seasons you will be better able to put to good use the knowledge obtained from him, and what you have learned yourself.

Faults that Will Appear

Some pairs may produce young faulty in head, or flat on back, or over-prominent in front or over-thin in front ; others bad in wing carriage, or maybe a little leggy, or not carrying the tail straight from the body but with a tendency to droop downwards, of perhaps inclined to split at the end, a failing termed " fish-tailed ".

Others may fail in colour and quality, and may even be far removed from the true type. Again, they may be weak in carriage of the head. These, with many others, are faults from which you will see how they have thrown on the average, for it is next to impossible to get all young from any given pair anything like equal in all points. And one may always expect some weeds which should be sold at the first chance. Never imagine these wasters will improve.

In some instances you must use caution, as, for example, when any bird may have received unwelcome attention from its parents and been plucked in the nest. If such are bred from typical parents they may turn out all right and repay you to keep. After another good moult they may mature into one of your best exhibition specimens, or if not up to show standard they may prove valuable stock birds.

Often at shows I have been asked : " What do you think I should get by pairing up those two birds ? " I have found in many instances the birds indicated were utterly unsuitable to be paired together, both having in a marked degree the same faults visible to an experienced eye.

On such an important point as this you cannot be too particular, and you must give careful study to the selection of your breeding pairs. Go carefully over your stock, and make up your mind which pairs you would like to put together.

B.F.C.C. Standard Comparison

Run them into a show cage, and pay marked attention to all the points laid down in the B.F.C.C. standard. See wherein they answer favourably to those points, and where they fail. Look carefully at their heads. If both are flat they will not do ; but if the one is a little flat but large in head, while the other is round and rather small, all well and good.

Next look at their necks, backs, wings, tails, size of body, length of leg, quality and colour of feather, general make-up and type. It is seldom you will find two birds equal in type or in other points, and, as already stated, if two birds have the same faults visible, try and get other partners for them.

Never pair two birds together showing the same faults unless absolutely forced to do so, as by so doing you cannot expect to get the progeny free from the same faults. Often enough they show up in a much worse degree.

Counterbalance Faults

Always try to mate birds so that each counterbalances any slight faults in the other. We will, for example, take a yellow cock, with a nice small, round head, fine neck, well-filled back, well laid-on wings, nice compact tail, graceful type, nice full breast, and with a jaunty carriage, close-fitting feathers on thighs and down towards the vent, and legs of medium length.

We have here a bird nearly perfect, but he may be a little washed out in colour, and have his feathers a little open (frilling at breast) and not fitting close enough. Also, he may carry his tail a little low and not in a straight line from the rise over the shoulder.

Now you see wherein this bird fails, and you can proceed to find a partner for him, say a buff hen. She must also be close, smooth, and of good quality of feather, with her tail carried straight out from the body, or if inclined to hold her tail a little up, so much the better.

Choose Hens Perfect in Type

You need not be so particular regarding head, etc., as the cock will balance matters here ; but always try and get the hen as perfect in every point as possible, especially so in any feature where a fault can be seen in the cock.

I have no hesitation whatever in saying that if you want to breed a good bird, you must see to it that the hen is perfect in type and quality, as her offspring resembles her most in these points. They take more after the cock bird in matters of size, etc. I trust I have made my point clear—that each weakness or fault in your stock birds should be counterbalanced in its mate.

At the same time always keep a watchful eye to make sure that the blood of each bird blends with the other, and that the type is in keeping with the standard which all breeders must have engraved firmly on their minds. To do so, keep the proof model sent out by the B.F.C.C. pasted in your stud book.

The stud book is another important matter where pedigree breeding is carried on. There are many on the market, but the best is published by *Cage Birds.**

The Value of a Stud Book

A stud book properly kept is a great help in establishing a superior strain. Each pair should be numbered, the number being stuck on the cage front, and particulars of the breeding pair entered in the stud book under the number corresponding.

Pay particular attention to jotting down all faults in the parents. The good points will look after themselves. Should the progeny have a fault similar to that in the cock, go back to his parents, and see if you have the same fault marked against either of them. By this method you will be able to trace a fault back for generations from either the cock or the hen.

This will ensure thorough control over

* *Cage Birds* Breeding Room Register. Obtainable from the publishers of this book. Price 1/8d post paid.

your breeding operations, and you will be able more certainly to shape your strain as regards the type, character, colour and quality of the young each pair should produce.

Should you introduce fresh blood, try and get it from a breeder whose strain of birds you are acquainted with. If possible, when introducing an outside cross, I always do so by purchasing a cock bird. Knowing the full pedigree of your hens, stick to them as the foundation of your strain, and any fault bred in from the cock is noticed earlier than when bred from the hen, should she be an outcross.

CHAPTER VIII

HOW TO MATE UP

BIRDS, like ourselves, are differently constituted, and vary very much in temper and disposition. Therefore it is well to study their peculiarities fully before finally attempting to pair up any couple. Don't run them together for good and all. Allow them a little courtship.

You can do this either by using a double breeding cage with a partition between, or by putting each in a separate show cage and placing the cages end on across the shelf, with the drinkers facing alternate ways. Then divide off each pair with a piece of cardboard cut the length and height of the cages.

Let them remain for a few days. Then, whenever you have some time to spare, run them together. Pay particular attention how they agree. If any are particularly quarrelsome, separate them immediately and house them as before.

As the old song says : " Absence makes

the heart grow fonder ", and I have found it so regarding our little favourites. When next run together they are quite friendly and afterwards proved a most affectionate pair.

I always adopt the above precaution, knowing the Border Fancy is of a determined nature, very active and strong in wing, and when two strange birds are put together suddenly they are apt to injure each other.

Egg-Binding and its Treatment

As soon as the season has reached the latter end of March, if the weather is favourable, one may begin to think of breeding. Winds blowing from the east, however, are very harmful. Sharp and piercing, they penetrate through any badly-fitting window or door, or even a small opening in either ceiling or floor, with the result that hens catch a chill.

If such a chill is allowed to develop they become so weak and prostrate that they have no strength to lay their eggs, becoming what is known as egg-bound. The general symptoms noticed are that the hen becomes dull and listless and sits with her feathers all ruffled up.

Once you are satisfied a hen is egg-bound take her gently in your hand, blow up the feathers at the vent (which you will find very much enlarged) and let three drops of the best olive oil, which has been warmed to blood heat, fall on the vent. Gently rub it in with your finger, letting a little find its way into the vent.

Should she not lay in a few hours, catch her again, and hold her over a cupful of hot water, keeping the fingers a little open so as the steam may play well over the abdomen and vent. Then roll her up in flannel which has been well warmed, and place her before a good fire, taking care to leave breathing space at the end.

In severe cases you may need to administer two drops of castor oil, also slightly warmed, into her beak, but let this be only a last resort.

After she has laid, which she may do in the flannel, put her into her cage, and give her a little bread soaked in warm milk with a little sugar and maw seed sprinkled over it, and she may lay the rest of her clutch all safely.

A frequent cause of egg-binding is due to the fact that hens are over-fat at the time of being paired up. Therefore watch the condition of your hens' abdomens.

Some hens that have been egg-bound are often troubled by irregularity with their eggs, sometimes laying only one egg, or even dropping an occasional egg from the perch, while others may lay the full number, but will not sit.

So I am convinced that when once a hen is egg-bound, there is always some more or less serious internal weakness. Therefore prevention is far better than cure, and the surest way to prevent its occurrence is not to pair birds up until the hens are thoroughly fit, which will be about the second week in April. The weather then is usually milder and more settled. It is seldom indeed we find a hen egg-bound after the soft May breezes blow.

The Breeding Cage

The breeding cages I find best for Borders are those of the orthodox box pattern. The fancier may like to make his own cages, but I find it does not pay.

They can be bought very cheaply, and professionally-constructed cages are much better made than the average affair put together by an amateur.

The cage I use is a single breeding size, length 20 inches, height 16 inches, and width 10 inches.

I use a nest of appropriate size for my birds. A large nest should not be used, as the Border is a small Canary and cannot sit comfortably in too large a nest. In a large receptacle she does not cover the eggs so well as when a small nest is employed.

See that your room is thoroughly dry, as nothing is so injurious to the health of birds as damp.

Ventilation should be carefully studied and intake and outlet ventilators are most desirable, the former being fitted low down and covered with fine zinc gauze, and the latter high up to allow the egress of all foul air, all also covered with perforated sheet zinc.

There should be no strongly moving current of air allowed to pass about the bird-room or chills may be produced. The aim should be to arrange wholly adequate ventilation without a suspicion of draught, and the test that ventilation is all it should be will be decided by one's nose on entering the room in the morning.

CHAPTER IX

HATCHING AND REARING

YOU should know when a hen is about to hatch her eggs by referring to your diary. A supply of egg food must be given her, made as follows :—Crush three rich tea biscuits and add one hard-boiled egg made fine by passing through a fine sieve. Add also a little brown sugar and a pinch of maw seed.

Mix well together and give each pair about a teaspoonful the night before the young are due to hatch. Increase the quantity each day as the young get older. Egg food should be given fresh three times a day if possible, all stale food being thrown out. You should now add a small quantity of hemp-seed, the supply of which should be increased as the birds grow.

When the young are three days old, I place between the wires a little green food. I like dandelion for the first round, lettuce for the second, and by the time the third lot of chicks are due there is always an unlimited supply of seeding grasses available, such as chickweed, mouse-ear, etc. Another useful help in the way of change is German summer rape. This can be prepared as follows :—Place the required quantity in a saucepan, boil it for ten minutes, strain through a sieve and dry by rubbing it well on a coarse towel, when it is ready for use.

This makes the hen attend to her young more often and is a good condiment at all times, both for old and young. When the young are about to leave the nest, keep your cage bottoms scrupulously clean. Usually there is a lot of stale food and droppings about and young birds are apt to pick them up. This frequently causes mischief with their bowels and disaster quickly follows.

Disinfect the Bird-Room

It is surprising how quickly a bird-room will begin to smell unpleasant if neglected or poorly ventilated, especially when the weather is warm. Therefore the motto should always be " cleanliness first ". Keep your room well treated with a good disinfectant, many of which are constantly being advertised in *Cage Birds*.

When the young have attained the age of three weeks, and are nicely feathered, the hen will be eager to build her second nest. Therefore arrange another nest for her. You must keep a strict eye on her at this period to see she does not pluck the young. Some hens are terrors in this respect, and when a hen once starts plucking there is little hope of curing her.

I have always found it best, when a hen starts plucking, to take the young from her and place them in a nursery cage, hanging it in front of the breeding cage. The parents will then feed through the wires all right. Should the parents forsake them, then put them back for an hour or so at a time, until they are at an age when a good feeding cock will take them over.

A good feeding cock is worth his weight in gold when the young have just left the nest. At the age of 28 days the babies should be able to fend for themselves.

Changing the Food

After the young birds have been removed from their parents, supply them with egg food as before until they are at least six weeks old, for too sudden a change of food often proves fatal. Therefore be cautious how you take them off the soft food, gradually reducing the quantity while increasing the supply of crushed canary hemp and boiled rape.

They should be able to crack the canary seed about this time, but the hemp is too much for them ; indeed, I may say that I always use the hemp crushed when giving it to my birds. Offer them a little green food but be careful. Green food has a tendency to relax the bowels, and too much may set up inflammation. Keep your eye on the condition of the bowels, and increase or reduce the supply accordingly.

Young birds at this time delight in a bath, so you can, with every confidence, supply one on nice warm days—twice a week if possible. Never, however, let them bathe on dull, damp days, or at any time after mid-day. This gives them time to preen and dry themselves before they settle down for a sleep.

By this time they are ready for the flights and from five to six may be kept together. But on the first sign of any plucking, the culprit should be removed into a single cage, as they very soon learn this vice from one another, so that damaged wings and tails result.

The Single Nestling

During the rounds you may possibly have a nest with only one youngster. When this occurs, it is better to remove it to a nest with others, or place a chick from another nest beside it. Seldom is a solitary youngster successfully reared.

A youngster transferred in this way must be marked, unless it be of another variety, say, a clear amongst greens or vice versa. It can be marked by means of a small piece of rubber tubing placed on the leg, and when old enough to be distinguished, the tubing can be removed.

After the youngsters are firmly on a hard seed diet, you must enter in your stud book the colour, sex and type of each, together with particulars of any other feature by which you are sure to know them. You must also record against them the number of the pair from which they were bred, for future reference.

Of course, where birds are marked you

have only to jot down the precise markings, as out of a season's breeding it is seldom we have two birds alike. The same applies to ticked specimens. With Clears, Greens and Cinnamons, although the type, colour, and length of body, wings, and tail are much at variance, to make sure of pedigree equip the youngsters with rings of different colour. An alternative plan is to paste a slip of paper on the front of the cage with the particulars and number of the pair they were bred from.

Should a number of the progeny die from any pair of birds, try and find out the cause of death and enter it accordingly. And while on the subject of records, I may add that it is well to work out the financial state of the season's breeding. Jot down all your sales and income from prize money, etc., and on the other side keep a record of expenditure.

CHAPTER X

CARE DURING THE MOULT

WHEN we want rich quality of feather in our Borders—and it is a fundamentally important feature in this breed—we must have our stock in a good state of health before the moult sets in. In my opinion, fresh green food, especially the wild, seeding plants, do no harm, but on the contrary the birds receive much benefit from them, both as regards quality, colour and health.

Run your eye carefully over your stock and select all those which you think conform to show standard. All the remainder, except those you may require for stock purposes, should be sold as early as possible so as to provide more room for the exhibition stock. Overcrowding at this time is detrimental.

All specimens intended for show should be moulted in separate cages, where room and financial considerations will allow. See that these cages are well washed out.

This is the exhibitor's " honey harvest ",
and the whole success of a show season
hangs on a successful moult quickly carried
through.

Where the Early Bird Scores

The moulting season begins in July for
early-hatched young, and may not finish
until December in the case of really late-
hatched birds. I am a firm believer in
three nests only, so I neither start early
nor continue late.   The two first rounds of
youngsters always enjoy the best moult,
and thereby make the best and most satis-
factory show birds. With late-bred birds
you have a difficulty in getting them to
finish the moult.

They may finish in a way, but are always
more or less patchy in colour and never so
level and fine in feather as their more
fortunate brothers and sisters whom Nature
favoured by sending into the moult a few
months earlier when the weather was
warmer. The moult is undoubtedly the
most critical period of a bird's life ; indeed,
its whole after-life depends on it.

A prolonged and faulty moult is the same
to a young bird as distemper is to a young

dog, and, therefore, quite as liable to
produce the same results if neglected. I
have found a young cock which has had
a prolonged moult is rarely capable of
fertilising his first nest of eggs, and some
do not even impregnate a single egg in a
season. Further, if they do their progeny
are mostly puny things.

Take again the case of the hens that
pass through the same protracted moult.
Many of them never lay a single egg, and
if they do hatch out young, they make very
indifferent mothers.

Now if either of these is kept until
another year, and has a good and quick
moult, you will have the exactly opposite
results. I might go on to cite many more
cases to illustrate the ill-effects of a bad
moult, but the above will suffice to show
how important it is to pay marked and
strict attention to all birds at this time.
Any neglect of duty then is sure to be
attended by much vexation afterwards.

First Symptoms of the Moult

The birds show the first signs of the
approaching moult by becoming a little
drowsy and listless and inclined to toss

their seed about for something which, seemingly, cannot be found.

To the beginner it looks as if some illness is overtaking them, which is not far wrong. The birds themselves do not seem to know exactly what is upsetting them. When the above symptoms are observed the best thing one can do is to provide an entire change of diet.

Put them on to boiled rape with a little ground sulphur sprinkled over it. A few groats should also be given among the shell gravel in the bottom of the cage. The gravel should be replenished twice a week if possible.

Never forget to be up early at moulting time in order to prepare the birds' breakfast, which should consist of half-a-teaspoonful of egg-food with four drops of chemical food added. Also give in the water a pinch of salts for two days. Change the water and give it clear for two days, and then add a piece of sulphate of iron the size of a split-pea. The iron stains the drinkers and must not be used in any glasses you intend to use in your show cages.

In a few days, if your birds are in good

health, several loose feathers should be found in the bottom of the cage. In old birds they will be tail and flight feathers as they always throw such feathers first. A few feathers down the breast will also appear disarranged, and in a few days these also will be shed.

In their place you will observe two narrow strips of feathers more brilliant and deeper in hue. These are the new feathers coming. The old ones, having faded in colour, look pale and washed out beside the latest arrivals.

A Safe and Speedy Moult

If the feathers appear in this way it is a sign things are progressing well. The more vivid in colour these stripes become, expanding towards the back and also appearing on the point of the wing, the better sign it is of your birds enjoying a safe and speedy moult.

Keep them warm at this period. Great care should be taken to avoid all draughts. Do not open the windows, or give the bath on raw, foggy days. Chills acquired at this period either result in a lingering illness, termed " stuck in moult ", or in death.

If your birds are all progressing favourably, when they appear to be a little more free in their movements, hopping from perch to perch as you handle their cage, stop the boiled rape, and feed as follows until they are gone three weeks in moult (when it may be necessary to change their diet somewhat so as to give to their feathers that fine glossy shade so much sought after by exhibitors).

Blow out their seed boxes every morning and refill with fresh canary seed, which should at this time be the best procurable. It often happens that your birds are good judges of seed and refuse to eat poor stuff.

When Birds are off Colour

You may find they shell a boxful, but actually eat very little. Whenever you find them acting in this manner, check over the seed and look to their health, as this is often the first sign of a bird being out of sorts. If you think your seed is at fault, change it.

If, on the other hand, you see clearly that your bird is out of sorts, give twelve drops of magnesia in the drinking water, and if the trouble is not of long standing, two days will be quite sufficient to use it.

Select a good seed, and every day fill your boxes with it. Every other day add to it a third of German summer rape. On the days you are not giving the rape, give half-a-teaspoonful of egg-food, and, once a week (say, on Tuesday) some hemp seed in the cage bottom amongst the gravel I like them to hunt for this.

On Thursday give a few groats, and on Sunday a little maw and linseed in the corner of the seed boxes. Give no green food after the days become colder, and the birds are fairly into the moult unless, once a week, perhaps, for a change some seeded grasses, chickweed, or mouse-ear. This should be gathered and laid up to dry a few days before being fed to the birds.

Also place between the wires a small piece of boiled carrot, and keep a small piece of mutton suet there for them to peck at. Give the bath once a week now on bright days. Add to it a little essence of quassia, the quantity depending on the size of bath used.

A good - sized cage should be kept

especially for bathing purposes, and after use it should be washed out and allowed to dry. When dry, keep it covered with a piece of paper so as to exclude all dust. You will find the use of the bath a great help in promoting the growth of the new feathers. Rain-water is preferable, but it must be clean.

While your birds are in the bath cage, clean out the living cage thoroughly. Sponge out all dust you can see on seedbox or wires. Also attend to the perches and, when dirty, wash with hot water. The cages will then be fit for the return of their inmates.

CHAPTER XI

PREPARATION FOR SHOW

BY this time you will have a good idea which of your birds are going to turn out fit for show, and you should place them in single cages with all their seed boxes facing outwards so that you can feed them without lifting down the cages.

Keep them out of strong light so that their new plumage is not affected in any way.

Any birds not moulting freely at this period should be changed to a warm living room, covered up with flannel, given linseed tea to drink, and then returned to their own room and fed as formerly. This treatment will often start them moulting freely.

Clean and Paint the Show Cages

Having all your birds in moult, and some of them fast finishing, you must give attention to your show cages and travelling cases. Have all cleaned, washed, dried and blacked all over, both wood and wires.

The rules of the B.F.C.C. say cages must be black, with no distinguishing marks or coloured perches. Some fanciers do not take the trouble to wash and touch up their cages for every show, which is a grave mistake and places their birds at a great disadvantage alongside others turned out clean and staged to perfection. In keen competition the former have little chance, even though two birds may be of equal merit. A dirty cage will not pass.

I have often been asked by novices how they can get their birds into condition and keep them so, imagining that there is some special food which will effect this. When told that nothing but cleanliness makes the difference they seem surprised.

Sometimes one will retort : " It is not the cage I sent to win a prize. It is the bird inside it ". " Quite true up to a point ", you reply, " but look how well the winning birds are staged in spotless condition. That can never be done in a dirty cage ".

Wherever the fancier's spirit is strong enough there is always sufficient time to go thoroughly over everything that will help your birds to succeed on the show bench. It is often through being lukewarm that some fanciers fail.

Novices will find that a little extra care and attention will often repay them double. Indeed, it is only through hard work and attending to the little details that we are able to mount up a few more rungs of the ladder to success. The only way to advance in any hobby is by having your plans well and soundly laid.

After you have all your cages and cases ready, your birds may be finishing up in moult. Never send out a bird to a show until quite hard and finished in head. Otherwise in a cold, draughty hall it may receive a chill which may put it out of competition for the remainder of the season. Always remember that it is the perfect and most hard and healthy bird that wins.

Treatment of Show Birds

Immediately you receive your birds home from a show, if not too late at night, have them unpacked in the kitchen, or living room, where there is a fire. Let them stand a few minutes before giving them anything to eat or drink, to see if they are all right.

If they are fit and hopping about in a lively way, give them their water slightly warmed and a little bread and milk with maw seed sprinkled over it. You may now take them into the bird-room if they arrive during the daytime, and on a clear dry day place them in a bath cage and allow them to bathe. If in good health and spirits they will enjoy this.

Always remember to give the bathing water a little above the temperature of the bird-room. Any that will not wash should be gently sprayed. After they have had their bath, return them to their stock cages, and keep them out of draughts.

Any bird a little out of sorts upon arrival from a show, and inclined to sit humped up with ruffled feathers, may be given five drops of whisky in its drinking water. Also keep in readiness some old, stale sponge cake. Cut a slice the thickness of the space between the wires in the cage. Dip this into sherry wine and sugar, and if nothing serious is the matter this will put the bird right. Do not allow any ailing birds to bathe or they may develop a chill.

Try and keep your show birds quite clean, so as to do away with hand-washing as far as possible. Birds hand-washed too often tend to lose the natural bloom of feather and can never compete successfully against one fresh out at its first show.

The novice should never attempt to wash a bird until he has seen one or two practical demonstrations, as it is a very trying ordeal, and if not well handled the bird may be spoiled for the season.

Most Cage Bird Societies have their " washing nights ", when some prominent member will handle the bird in the wash and explain the various points in cleaning, rinsing and drying. All Border fanciers, therefore, should join their nearest society, attend all the meetings, especially on washing night, and keep their eyes and ears open for everything that will help with their hobby.

Evils of Over-Showing

Never, on any account, over-show a good bird, or you may live to rue it. No doubt, when one has an all-round show bird, and especially if it has already brought a little fame to you, it is a great temptation to turn it out at every show, thinking you are sure to win every time.

You may do well at the first show, but the continued strain upon the bird's nerves and constitution will tell, with the result that it becomes dull and listless, dry in feather, and all out of condition, and in such a state it cannot be expected to win a prize.

Study the Judges

Another vital point in successful showing which must always be particularly studied is to discover what type and size of bird the judge favours, and select accordingly. There is a great difference of opinion among judges, although we have all the same model to work to. Judges do not all see eye to eye. Each has his own particular type, fads and fancies.

It pays to jot down in your notebook for future reference each judge's fads, as we may term them. When you see a judge engaged for a show you have only to refer to your notebook, and then select a team to send under him, suitable to *his* standard.

This can only be done by attending all the shows within reasonable distance. One can always learn a lot at shows. You will there meet fanciers to whom it is a pleasure to talk, and who are quite willing to help the beginner. You will also meet fanciers (so - called at least) who are always grumbling at the judge's decision. These are to be avoided.

In this pastime of exhibiting Canaries, we are bound to lose sometimes, and it leads nowhere to abuse the winner, or the judge, for that matter, when we fail to get the red ticket. It is better to keep a cool head, an even temper, and a quiet tongue, and never accuse the judge of holding a biased opinion towards the successful exhibitor. Above all, show true sportsmanship, otherwise the Fancy in general has no room for you.

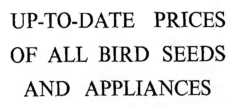

BOOKS ON BIRDKEEPING AND AQUARIA

BUDGERIGARS

	Price	By Post
" The Cult of the Budgerigar "	15/-	15/9
" The Budgerigar in Captivity "	2/6	2/9
" Colour Breeding in Budgerigars "	1/-	1/2
" The Budgerigar Breeding and Show Register " ..	1/6	1/8
" Budgerigar Matings and Colour Expectations " ..	10/6	11/-
" Budgerigars and How to Breed Them "	3/6	3/9
" In-breeding Budgerigars "	3/-	3/3
" Talking Budgerigars "	1/-	1/2
" Budgerigar Breeders' Pedigree Forms " per book,	6d.	8d.

CANARIES

" Guide to Canary Breeding "	8/6	9/-
" Canary Breeding for Beginners "	2/6	2/9
" Norwich Canaries "	1/6	1/9
" The Yorkshire Canary "	3/6	3/9
" The Roller Canary "	3/-	3/3
" Canary Breeding Room Register "	1/6	1/8

FOREIGN BIRDS

" Foreign Birds for Garden Aviaries "	10/6	11/-

VARIOUS

" Breeding British Birds "	3/6	3/9
" Questions Answered About Cage Birds " ..	3/6	3/8
" Wartime Feeding of Cage Birds "	1/-	1/2
" Bird Ailments and Accidents "	3/6	3/10
" Wild Plants and Seeds for Birds "	2/6	2/9
" Mules and Hybrids "	3/6	3/10

THE " NUTSHELL " SERIES

No. 5.	The Canary	No. 25.	Insectivorous British Birds—Pt. I
10.	The Roller Canary	26.	Insectivorous British Birds—Pt. II
16.	Cockatiels		
17.	Grey Parrots	37.	Silkworms
20.	Waxbills		

Price 4d. each, by post 5d.

AQUARIA

First Steps in Aquarium Keeping
Hardy Reptiles and Amphibians
Live Foods for Aquarium Fishes

Garden Ponds
Aquatic Insects
Marsh Gardens
The Goldfish
Tropical Fishes
The Terrarium

Price 1/6 each, by post 1/8

Obtainable from all Newsagents or direct from the Publishers :
POULTRY WORLD LTD., DORSET HOUSE, STAMFORD ST., S.E.1